THE 30-MINUTE SHAKESPEARE

JULIUS CAESAR

"Nick Newlin's work as a teaching artist for Folger Education during the past thirteen years has provided students, regardless of their experience with Shakespeare or being on stage, a unique opportunity to tread the boards at the Folger Theatre. Working with students to edit Shakespeare's plays for performance at the annual Folger Shakespeare Festivals has enabled students to gain new insights into the Bard's plays, build their skills of comprehension and critical reading, and just plain have fun working collaboratively with their peers.

Folger Education promotes performance-based teaching of Shakespeare's plays, providing students with an interactive approach to Shakespeare's plays in which they participate in a close reading of the text through intellectual, physical, and vocal engagement. Newlin's *The 30-Minute Shakespeare* series is an invaluable resource for teachers of Shakespeare, and for all who are interested in performing the plays."

ROBERT YOUNG, PH.D.

DIRECTOR OF EDUCATION

FOLGER SHAKESPEARE LIBRARY

Julius Caesar: The 30-Minute Shakespeare
ISBN 978-1-935550-29-7

There is no royalty for performing *Julius Caesar: The 30-Minute Shakespeare* in a classroom or on a stage; however, permission must be obtained for all playscripts used by the actors. The publisher hereby grants unlimited photocopy permission for one series of performances to all acting groups that have purchased at least five (5) copies of the paperback edition, or one (1) copy of the downloadable PDF edition available for $12.95 from www.30MinuteShakespeare.com. If a group uses an eBook edition to stage a performance, post a comment to our Facebook page; we'd love to hear about it.

Cover design by Sarah Juckniess
Printed in the United States of America

Distributed by Consortium Book Sales & Distribution
www.cbsd.com

NICOLO WHIMSEY PRESS
www.30MinuteShakespeare.com

Art Director: Sarah Juckniess
Managing Editors: Katherine Little, Leah Gordon

THE TRAGEDIE of
JULIUS CÆSAR

THE 30-MINUTE SHAKESPEARE

Written by WILLIAM SHAKESPEARE

Abridged AND Edited
by NICK NEWLIN

Nicolo Whimsey
Press

Brandywine, MD

To my grandmother,
Elizabeth Battles Newlin
("Gammy")

whose love was constant
as the northern star

Special thanks to Joanne Flynn, Bill Newlin, Eliza Newlin Carney, William and Louisa Newlin, Michael Tolaydo, Hilary Kacser, Sarah Juckniess, Katherine Little, Eva Zimmerman, Leah Gordon, Tanya Tolchin, Frank Harris, Julie Schaper and all of Consortium, Leo Bowman and the students, faculty, and staff at Banneker Academic High School, and Robert Young Ph.D. and the Folger Shakespeare Library, especially the wonderful Education Department.

✷ TABLE OF CONTENTS

✳ NO EXPERIENCE NECESSARY

I was not a big "actor type" in high school, so if you weren't either, or if the young people you work with are not, then this book is for you. Whether or not you work with "actor types," you can use this book to stage a lively and captivating thirty-minute version of a Shakespeare play. No experience is necessary.

When I was about eleven years old, my parents took me to see Shakespeare's *Two Gentlemen of Verona,* which was being performed as a Broadway musical. I didn't comprehend every word I heard, but I was enthralled with the language, the characters, and the story, and I understood enough of it to follow along. From then on, I associated Shakespeare with *fun*.

Of course Shakespeare is fun. The Elizabethan audiences knew it, which is one reason he was so popular. It didn't matter that some of the language eluded them. The characters were passionate and vibrant, and their conflicts were compelling. Young people study Shakespeare in high school, but more often than not they read his work like a text book and then get quizzed on academic elements of the play, such as plot, theme, and vocabulary. These are all very interesting, but not nearly as interesting as standing up and performing a scene! It is through performance that the play comes alive and all its "academic" elements are revealed. There is nothing more satisfying to a student or teacher than the feeling of "owning" a Shakespeare play, and that can only come from performing it.

But Shakespeare's plays are often two or more hours long, making the performance of an entire play almost out of the question. One can perform a single scene, which is certainly a good start, but what about the story? What about the changes a character goes through as the play progresses? When school groups perform one scene unedited, or when they lump several plays together, the audience can get lost. This is why I have always preferred to tell the story of the play.

The 30-Minute Shakespeare gives students and teachers a chance to get up on their feet and act out a Shakespeare play in half an hour, using his language. The emphasis is on key scenes, with narrative bridges between scenes to keep the audience caught up on the action. The stage directions are built into this script so that young actors do not have to stand in one place; they can move and tell the story with their actions as well as their words. And it can all be done in a classroom during class time!

That is where this book was born: not in a research library, a graduate school lecture, a professional stage, or even an after-school drama club. All of the play cuttings in *The 30-Minute Shakespeare* were first rehearsed in a D.C. public high school English class, and performed successfully at the Folger Shakespeare Library's annual Secondary School Shakespeare Festival. The players were not necessarily "actor types." For many of them, this was their first performance in a play.

Something almost miraculous happens when students perform Shakespeare. They "get" it. By occupying the characters and speaking the words out loud, students gain a level of understanding and appreciation that is unachievable by simply reading the text. That is the magic of a performance-based method of learning Shakespeare, and this book makes the formerly daunting task of staging a Shakespeare play possible for anybody.

With *The 30-Minute Shakespeare* book series I hope to help teachers and students produce a Shakespeare play in a short amount of time, thus jump-starting the process of discovering the beauty, magic, and fun of the Bard. Plot, theme, and language reveal themselves through the performance of these half-hour play cuttings, and everybody involved receives the priceless gift of "owning" a piece of Shakespeare. The result is an experience that is fun and engaging, and one that we can all carry with us as we play out our own lives on the stages of the world.

NICK NEWLIN

Brandywine, MD

March 2010

CHARACTERS IN THE PLAY

The following is a list of characters that appear in this cutting of Julius Caesar.

For the full breakdown of characters, see Sample Program.

SOOTHSAYER

CHORUS

JULIUS CAESAR: A great Roman general

CALPURNIA: Caesar's wife

ANTONY: A loyal friend of Caesar

BRUTUS: A high ranking nobleman

PORTIA: Brutus's wife

CASSIUS

CASCA

CINNA

DECIUS BRUTUS

METELLUS CIMBER

TREBONIUS

CINNA

(Cassius through Cinna: Patricians; conspirators against Caesar)

CITIZENS

CINNA THE POET

GHOST OF CAESAR

PINDARUS: Slave to Cassius

TITINIUS **MESSALA** **CLITUS** **VOLUMNIUS** **STRATO**	Officers and soldiers in the armies of Brutus and Cassius

NARRATOR

✷ SCENE 1. (ACT I, SCENE II)

A public place.

Enter NARRATOR *from stage rear, coming downstage center. Enter* CHORUS *from stage right and stage left, making a "V" shape behind* NARRATOR.

NARRATOR

A soothsayer warns Caesar of a dangerous day for him. Cassius is afraid that Caesar will become king and urges Brutus to oppose him. An ill wind blows. (CHORUS *wave arms to emulate wind.)*

Exit NARRATOR *stage left.*

Enter SOOTHSAYER *from stage left, blindly feeling his way forward. Enter* CINNA THE POET *from stage left to guide* SOOTHSAYER *to* CHORUS *at center stage.*

Enter JULIUS CAESAR, ANTONY, CALPURNIA, PORTIA, DECIUS BRUTUS, BRUTUS, CASSIUS, CASCA, TREBONIUS, *and* METELLUS CIMBER *from stage right.*

At CAESAR'S *entrance,* CHORUS *hum flourish.*

CAESAR

Calpurnia!

CASCA *(silencing crowd with a wave of his hand)*

Peace, ho! Caesar speaks.

CAESAR *(gesturing)*
Calpurnia!

CALPURNIA
Here, my lord.

CAESAR
Antonius!

ANTONY
Caesar, my lord?

SOOTHSAYER
Caesar!
Beware the ides of March.
(louder and with more intensity) Beware the ides of March.

CAESAR
He is a dreamer; let us leave him: pass.

Exit ALL *stage left except* BRUTUS *and* CASSIUS.

STAGE RIGHT CHORUS *hum flourish.*

STAGE LEFT CHORUS *(shouting)*
Hail Caesar!

BRUTUS
What means this shouting? I do fear, the people
Choose Caesar for their king.

CASSIUS
Ay, do you fear it?
Then must I think you would not have it so.

BRUTUS

What is it that you would impart to me?

CASSIUS

I was born free as Caesar; so were you:
We both have fed as well, and we can both
Endure the winter's cold as well as he:
And this man
Is now become a god.

STAGE RIGHT CHORUS *(shouting)*

Hail Caesar!

CASSIUS

Why, man, he doth bestride the narrow world
Like a Colossus, and we petty men
Walk under his huge legs and peep about
To find ourselves dishonorable graves.
Men at some time are masters of their fates:
The fault, dear Brutus, is not in our stars,
But in ourselves, that we are underlings.
Brutus—

CHORUS *(shouting)*

Brutus!

CASSIUS

—and Caesar.

CHORUS *(shouting)*

Caesar!

CASSIUS

What should be in that 'Caesar'?
Why should that name be sounded more than yours?

BRUTUS

My noble friend, chew upon this:
Brutus had rather be a villager
Than to repute himself a son of Rome
Under these hard conditions as this time
Is like to lay upon us.

CHORUS *hum flourish.*

Re-enter CAESAR, ANTONY, CALPURNIA, PORTIA, DECIUS BRUTUS, BRUTUS, CASSIUS, CASCA, TREBONIUS, *and* METELLUS CIMBER *from stage left.*

CAESAR

Antonius!

ANTONY

Caesar?

CAESAR

Let me have men about me that are fat;
Yond Cassius has a lean and hungry look;
He thinks too much: such men are dangerous.
He hears no music.

CHORUS *(echoing)*

No music!

CAESAR

Seldom he smiles.
Such men as he be never at heart's ease
Whiles they behold a greater than themselves,
And therefore are they very dangerous.

CHORUS *(echoing)*

Dangerous!

CHORUS *hum flourish.*

Exit CAESAR, ANTONY, CALPURNIA, PORTIA, DECIUS BRUTUS, TREBONIUS, *and* METELLUS CIMBER *stage right.*

CASCA *(to* BRUTUS*)*

I saw Mark Antony offer Caesar a crown; he put it by, but, to my thinking, he was very loath to lay his fingers off it. And still as he refused it, the rabblement hooted and clapped their chapped hands.

STAGE LEFT CHORUS *hoot;* STAGE RIGHT CHORUS *clap hands.*

Then Caesar fell down in the marketplace, and foamed at mouth, and was speechless.

BRUTUS

'Tis very like: he hath the falling sickness.

CASSIUS

No, Caesar hath it not; but you and I,
And honest Casca, we have the falling sickness.

CASCA

Farewell, both.

Exit **CASCA** *stage right.*

BRUTUS

For this time I will leave you too:
Tomorrow, I will wait for you.

CASSIUS

I will do so: till then, think of the world.

Exit BRUTUS *stage right.*

Well, Brutus, thou art noble; yet, I see,
Thy honorable metal may be wrought
From that it is disposed:
(taking a step toward audience)
For who so firm that cannot be seduced?
Caesar doth bear me hard; but he loves Brutus:
Caesar's ambition shall be glanced at:
And after this let Caesar seat him sure;
For we will shake him, or worse days endure.

Exit CASSIUS *stage left.* CHORUS *remain onstage.*

✶ **SCENE 2.** (ACT II, SCENE I)

Rome. BRUTUS'S *orchard.*

Enter NARRATOR *from stage rear, coming downstage center.*

NARRATOR

Brutus and the other conspirators decide to kill Caesar but spare Antony. Portia begs Brutus, her husband, to explain his change in mood. Storm clouds gather.

Exit NARRATOR *stage left.*

STAGE LEFT CHORUS *make sounds of thunder;* STAGE RIGHT CHORUS *make sounds of rain.*

Enter BRUTUS *from stage right.*

BRUTUS

It must be by his death: and for my part,
I know no personal cause to spurn at him,
But for the general. He would be crown'd:
It is the bright day that brings forth the adder;

STAGE RIGHT CHORUS *gesture upward;* STAGE LEFT CHORUS *gesture downward.*

Therefore think him as a serpent's egg
Which, hatch'd, would, as his kind, grow mischievous,
And kill him in the shell.

CHORUS *gesture in unison.*

SOUND OPERATOR *plays* Sound Cue #1 ("Knocking").

They are the faction. O conspiracy,
Where wilt thou find a cavern dark enough
To mask thy monstrous visage?

Enter from stage right the CONSPIRATORS: CASSIUS, CASCA, DECIUS BRUTUS, CINNA, METELLUS CIMBER, *and* TREBONIUS.

BRUTUS

Give me your hands all over, one by one.

CONSPIRATORS *bring hands in, forming a circle.*

CASSIUS

And let us swear our resolution.

CONSPIRATORS *remove hands from circle.*

DECIUS BRUTUS

Shall no man else be touch'd but only Caesar?

CASSIUS

Let Antony and Caesar fall together.

BRUTUS

Our course will seem too bloody, Caius Cassius,
To cut the head off and then hack the limbs,
For Antony is but a limb of Caesar:
Let's kill him boldly, but not wrathfully;
Which so appearing to the common eyes,
We shall be call'd purgers, not murderers.

CASSIUS

Yet I fear him;
For in the ingrafted love he bears to Caesar—

SOUND OPERATOR *plays* Sound Cue #2 ("Clock striking three").

CASSIUS

The clock hath stricken three.

TREBONIUS

'Tis time to part.

Exit **ALL** *but* **BRUTUS** *stage right.*

Exit **CHORUS**, *splitting down the middle to exit stage right and stage left.*

Enter **PORTIA** *from stage left.*

PORTIA

Brutus, my lord!

BRUTUS

Portia, what mean you? Wherefore rise you now?

PORTIA *(moving close to* **BRUTUS***)*

You've ungently, Brutus, stole from my bed:
And when I ask'd you what the matter was,
You stared upon me and stamp'd with your foot;
Dear my lord,
Make me acquainted with your cause of grief.

BRUTUS *(moving away from* **PORTIA** *toward stage right)*

I am not well in health, and that is all.

PORTIA

What, is Brutus sick,
And will he steal out of his wholesome bed,
To dare the vile contagion of the night
To add unto his sickness?

PORTIA *moves toward* BRUTUS.

No, my Brutus;
You have some sick offense within your mind,
Which I ought to know of *(touches his head)*
And, upon my knees,
I charm you, by my once-commended beauty,
That you unfold to me, yourself, your half,
Why you are heavy, and what men tonight
Have had to resort to you.

PORTIA *kneels.*

BRUTUS

Kneel not, gentle Portia.

BRUTUS *holds out his hand, which* PORTIA *clasps.* BRUTUS *helps* PORTIA *to her feet.*

PORTIA

I should not need, if you were gentle Brutus.
Dwell I but in the suburbs
Of your good pleasure?

PORTIA *turns her back to* BRUTUS, *facing stage left.*

If it be no more,
Portia is Brutus's harlot, not his wife.

BRUTUS *(turning* PORTIA *around)*

You are my true and honorable wife,
As dear to me as are the ruddy drops
That visit my sad heart.

PORTIA

If this were true, then should I know this secret.

BRUTUS *(looking up)*

O ye gods,
Render me worthy of this noble wife!
(gestures left) Portia, go in awhile;
And by and by thy bosom shall partake
The secrets of my heart.

BRUTUS *begins to exit stage left, crossing in front of* **PORTIA**. *He turns back toward her.*

Follow me, then.

Exit **BRUTUS** *stage left, with* **PORTIA** *following.*

✷ SCENE 3. (ACT II, SCENE II)

CAESAR'S *house.*

Enter **NARRATOR** *from stage rear, coming downstage center.*

NARRATOR

The dangerous day has arrived. Fearing for his safety, Caesar's wife, Calpurnia, urges him to stay home. But does he listen? No. *(pauses)* Typical man.

Exit **NARRATOR** *stage left.*

Enter **CHORUS** *from stage right and stage left, coming to center stage.*

CALPURNIA *(from offstage, yelling)*

Murder! Caesar!

STAGE LEFT CHORUS *make sounds of thunder;* **STAGE RIGHT CHORUS** *make sounds of rain.*

Enter **CAESAR**, *dressed in his nightgown, from stage right.*

STAGE RIGHT CHORUS *(shouting)*

Caesar!

STAGE LEFT CHORUS *(shouting)*

Murder!

CAESAR

Nor heaven nor earth have been at peace tonight:

Thrice hath Calpurnia in her sleep cried out,
'Help, ho! They murder Caesar!'

Enter CALPURNIA *from stage right.*

CALPURNIA *(approaching* CAESAR*)*
What mean you, Caesar? Think you to walk forth?
You shall not stir out of your house today.

CAESAR
Caesar shall forth: the things that threaten'd me
Ne'er look'd but on my back; when they shall see
The face of Caesar, they are vanished.

CALPURNIA
Caesar, I never stood on ceremonies,
Yet now they fright me.
A lioness hath whelped in the streets;

CHORUS, *in unison, shape hands into claws, bringing them to their bellies as if giving birth. They then lift their arms out, up, and over their heads from the centers of their bodies.*

And graves have yawn'd, and yielded up their dead;

CHORUS *stretch arms and hands toward the ground and then open their mouths and stretch arms upward.*

Horses did neigh,

CHORUS *mime holding reins, each member raising one foot.*

and dying men did groan,

CHORUS *clutch themselves tightly.*

And ghosts did shriek and squeal about the streets,

CHORUS *put hands around mouth and scream out loud.*

CALPURNIA, *startled, reacts physically to* **CHORUS'S** *scream.*

And I do fear them.

CAESAR

What can be avoided
Whose end is purposed by the mighty gods?
Yet Caesar shall go forth; for these predictions
Are to the world in general as to Caesar.

CALPURNIA

When beggars die, there are no comets seen;

CHORUS *mime begging, turning palms upward.*

The heavens themselves blaze forth the death
of princes.

CHORUS *raise arms up, wiggling their fingers to indicate stars.*

CAESAR

Cowards die many times before their deaths;
The valiant never taste of death but once.

CALPURNIA

Alas, my lord,
Your wisdom is consumed in confidence.
Do not go forth today: call it my fear
That keeps you in the house, and not your own.
Let me, upon my knee, prevail in this.

Enter **DECIUS BRUTUS** *from stage right.*

DECIUS BRUTUS

Caesar, all hail! Good morrow, worthy Caesar:
I come to fetch you to the senate-house.

CAESAR

Decius, go tell them Caesar will not come.

DECIUS BRUTUS

Most mighty Caesar, let me know some cause.

CAESAR

The cause is in my will: I will not come;
That is enough to satisfy the senate.
But for your private satisfaction,
Calpurnia here, my wife, stays me at home:
She dreamt tonight she saw my statue,

STAGE LEFT *and* STAGE RIGHT CHORUS *create identical tableaux of a citizen washing his hands in a statue fountain. (See Performance Notes.)*

Which, like a fountain with a hundred spouts,
Did run pure blood: and many lusty Romans
Came smiling, and did bathe their hands in it.

DECIUS BRUTUS

Your statue spouting blood in many pipes,
Signifies that from you great Rome shall suck
Reviving blood. The senate have concluded
To give this day a crown to mighty Caesar.
If Caesar hide himself, shall they not whisper
'Lo, Caesar is afraid'?

CAESAR

How foolish do your fears seem now, Calpurnia!
I am ashamed I did yield to them.
I will go.

CHORUS *break formation and join* DECIUS BRUTUS, *following* CAESAR *out. Exit* ALL *stage left.*

✱ SCENE 4. (ACT III, SCENE I)

Rome. Before the Capitol.

Enter NARRATOR *from stage rear, coming downstage center.*

NARRATOR

The conspirators surround Caesar. His wife was right: he should have stayed home.

Exit NARRATOR *stage left.*

Enter a crowd of CITIZENS, *among them* SOOTHSAYER, *who is helped onto the stage by* CINNA THE POET *from stage left.* CINNA THE POET *carries a notebook and begins writing poems once* SOOTHSAYER *is in place.*

SOUND OPERATOR *plays* Sound Cue #3 ("Drums").

Enter CAESAR, BRUTUS, CASSIUS, CASCA, DECIUS BRUTUS, METELLUS CIMBER, *and* TREBONIUS *from stage right.*

CAESAR *(to* SOOTHSAYER*)*

The ides of March are come.

SOOTHSAYER

Ay, Caesar; but not gone.

CAESAR *waves his arms to disperse* CITIZENS. *Exit* ALL *stage left, except for* CINNA THE POET, *who helps* SOOTHSAYER *to stage left.*

Exit CINNA THE POET *and* SOOTHSAYER *stage left.*

CAESAR

Are we all ready? What is now amiss
That Caesar and his senate must redress?

METELLUS CIMBER

Most high, most mighty, and most puissant Caesar,
Metellus Cimber throws before thy seat
An humble heart, for the appealing of my
banished brother.
(kneels)

CAESAR

I must prevent thee, Cimber.
These couchings and these lowly courtesies
Might fire the blood of ordinary men,
But I am constant as the northern star,
Of whose true-fix'd and resting quality
There is no fellow in the firmament.
That I was constant Cimber should be banish'd,
And constant do remain to keep him so.

DECIUS BRUTUS *(kneels)*

Great Caesar,—

CAESAR

Doth not Brutus bootless kneel?

CASCA

Speak, hands for me!

SOUND OPERATOR *plays* Sound Cue #4 ("Drums and recorder").

CASCA *stabs* **CAESAR** *in slow motion. The other* **CONSPIRATORS**, *also in slow motion, follow his action and stab at* **CAESAR**, *slowly killing him.* **BRUTUS**, *the last to attack, first recoils backward in horror, clutching his dagger, before coming up to* *stab* CAESAR. *Both* CAESAR *and* BRUTUS *freeze for an instant, looking into each other's eyes, with real time resuming as* BRUTUS *delivers the fatal thrust.*

The music stops, and there is a moment of silence as CAESAR *looks into* BRUTUS'S *eyes once more.*

CAESAR *(maintaining eye contact)*
Et tu, Brute!

CAESAR *looks out to audience.*

Then fall, Caesar.

CAESAR *dies.*

SOUND OPERATOR *plays* Sound Cue #5 ("Final drumbeat").

CINNA
Liberty! Freedom! Tyranny is dead!

CONSPIRATORS *(repeating)*
Tyranny is dead!

BRUTUS
Stoop, Romans, stoop,
And let us bathe our hands in Caesar's blood
Up to the elbows, and besmear our swords:
Then walk we forth, even to the marketplace,
And, waving our red weapons o'er our heads,
Let's all cry 'Peace, freedom, and liberty!'

CONSPIRATORS *(repeating)*
Peace! Freedom!
(lifting arms and swords upward) Liberty!
But here comes Antony.

Enter **ANTONY** *from stage left.*

Welcome, Mark Antony.

ANTONY *(kneeling by* **CAESAR'S** *body)*

O mighty Caesar! Dost thou lie so low?
(stands) Fare thee well.
I know not, gentlemen,
Who else must be let blood:
If I myself, there is no hour so fit
As Caesar's death hour.

ANTONY *opens his arms as if inviting* **CONSPIRATORS** *to stab him.*

BRUTUS *(putting his hand tentatively on* **ANTONY'S** *shoulder)*

O Antony, beg not your death of us.
Though now we must appear bloody and cruel,
Our hearts you see not; they are pitiful;
And pity to the general wrong of Rome—

ANTONY

I doubt not of your wisdom.
Let each man render me his bloody hand:
How like a deer, strucken by many princes,
Dost thou here lie!
(to **BRUTUS***)*
I am suitor that I may
Produce his body to the marketplace;
And in the pulpit, as becomes a friend,
Speak in the order of his funeral.

BRUTUS

You shall, Mark Antony.

CASSIUS

Brutus, a word with you.

CASSIUS *and* BRUTUS *move slightly stage right.*

(aside to BRUTUS*)* Do not consent
That Antony speak in his funeral:
Know you how much the people may be moved?

BRUTUS

By your pardon;
I will myself into the pulpit first,
And show the reason of our Caesar's death.

CASSIUS

I like it not.

BRUTUS

Mark Antony, here, take you Caesar's body.
You shall not in your funeral speech blame us.

Exit ALL *stage right, except* ANTONY.

ANTONY *(kneeling)*

O, pardon me, thou bleeding piece of earth,
That I am meek and gentle with these butchers!
(gestures toward CONSPIRATORS*)*
Thou art the ruins of the noblest man
That ever lived in the tide of times.
Woe to the hand that shed this costly blood!
Over thy wounds now do I prophesy,—
(standing) And Caesar's spirit, ranging for revenge,
Shall in these confines with a monarch's voice
Cry 'Havoc,' and let slip the dogs of war.

Exit ANTONY *stage right.*

CAESAR'S *body remains onstage during scene change.*

✷ **SCENE 5.** (ACT III, SCENE II)

The Forum.

Enter NARRATOR *from stage rear, coming downstage center.*

NARRATOR

Brutus justifies to the mob the killing of Caesar. Then Antony cleverly turns the crowd against Brutus and the conspirators. Politicians and their speeches—some things never change.

Exit NARRATOR *stage left.*

Enter CHORUS *from stage right and stage left, coming to center stage.*

Enter BRUTUS, CASSIUS, ANTONY, *and* CITIZENS *from stage rear. They stand center, slightly downstage of* CHORUS.

CITIZEN ONE

We will be satisfied!

CITIZEN TWO

Let us be satisfied!

CITIZEN THREE

The noble Brutus is ascended: Silence!

BRUTUS

Romans, countrymen, and lovers! If any dear friend of Caesar's demand why Brutus rose against Caesar, this is my answer:—Not that I loved Caesar less, but that I loved Rome more. As Caesar loved me, I weep for him; as he was valiant, I honor him: but, as he was ambitious, I slew him. Who is here so vile that will not love his country? If any, speak; for him have I offended. I pause for a reply.

STAGE RIGHT CHORUS

None, Brutus.

STAGE LEFT CHORUS

None!

BRUTUS

Then none have I offended. As I slew my best lover for the good of Rome, I have the same dagger for myself, when it shall please my country to need my death.

STAGE RIGHT CHORUS

Live, Brutus!

STAGE LEFT CHORUS

Live, live!

BRUTUS

Good countrymen,
Stay here with Antony:
And grace his speech
Tending to Caesar's glories; which Mark Antony,
By our permission, is allow'd to make.

Exit BRUTUS *stage left.*

CITIZEN ONE

Stay, ho! And let us hear Mark Antony.

CHORUS *(echoing)*
Antony!

CITIZEN FOUR
'Twere best he speak no harm of Brutus here.

CITIZEN ONE
This Caesar was a tyrant.

CHORUS *(echoing)*
Tyrant!

CITIZEN TWO
Peace! Let us hear what Antony can say.

CHORUS *(echoing)*
Antony!

ANTONY
Friends, Romans, countrymen, lend me your ears;
I come to bury Caesar, not to praise him.
The noble Brutus
Hath told you Caesar was ambitious:
And grievously hath Caesar answer'd it.
For Brutus is an honorable man;
Caesar hath brought many captives home to Rome
Whose ransoms did the general coffers fill:
Yet Brutus says he was ambitious;
And Brutus is an honorable man.
I thrice presented him a kingly crown,
Which he did thrice refuse: Was this ambition?
Yet Brutus says he was ambitious;
And, sure, he is an honorable man.
You all did love him once, not without cause:
O judgment! Thou art fled to brutish beasts,
And men have lost their reason.

CITIZEN ONE

Methinks there is much reason in his sayings.

CHORUS *(echoing)*

Reason!

CITIZEN TWO

Caesar has had great wrong.

CHORUS *(echoing)*

Wrong!

CITIZEN FOUR

He would not take the crown;
Therefore 'tis certain he was not ambitious.

CHORUS *(echoing)*

Not ambitious!

CITIZEN THREE

There's not a nobler man in Rome than Antony.

CHORUS *(echoing)*

Antony!

ANTONY

I fear I wrong the honorable men
Whose daggers have stabb'd Caesar;

CITIZEN FOUR

They were traitors.

CHORUS *(echoing)*

Traitors!

ANTONY

Then make a ring about the corpse of Caesar,
Shall I descend?

CHORUS

Come down.

ANTONY *comes downstage.*

CITIZEN FOUR

A ring; stand round.

CHORUS *(echoing)*

Round!

CITIZEN TWO

Room for Antony, most noble Antony.

CHORUS *(echoing)*

Most noble Antony!

ANTONY

If you have tears, prepare to shed them now.
You all do know this mantle:
Look, in this place ran Cassius's dagger through:
Through this the well-beloved Brutus stabb'd;
Mark how the blood of Caesar follow'd it,
This was the most unkindest cut of all;
Here is himself, marr'd, as you see, with traitors.

CITIZEN TWO

O noble Caesar!

CHORUS *(echoing)*

Caesar!

CITIZEN FOUR
O traitors, villains!

CHORUS *(echoing)*
Villains!

CITIZEN TWO
We will be revenged.

CHORUS *(echoing)*
Revenged!

STAGE RIGHT CHORUS *(raising fists up)*
Revenge!

STAGE LEFT CHORUS *(raising fists up)*
Seek!

STAGE RIGHT CHORUS *(raising fists up)*
Fire!

STAGE LEFT CHROUS *(raising fists up)*
Slay!

CHORUS *(raising fists up in unison)*
Let not a traitor live!

ANTONY
Sweet friends, let me not stir you up.
I am no orator, as Brutus is; but were I Brutus,
And Brutus Antony, there were an Antony
Would ruffle up your spirits and put a tongue
In every wound of Caesar that should move
The stones of Rome to rise and mutiny.

CHORUS

Seek the conspirators!

CITIZEN TWO

Most noble Caesar! We'll revenge his death.

CHORUS *(echoing)*

Revenge his death!

ANTONY

Here was a Caesar! When comes such another?

CITIZEN ONE

Never, never. Come, away, away!
We'll burn his body in the holy place,
And with the brands fire the traitors' houses.
Take up the body.

CHORUS *(echoing)*

Take up the body!

CITIZEN TWO

Go fetch fire.

CHORUS *(echoing)*

Fire!

Exit CITIZENS *with* CAESAR'S *body stage right.*

ANTONY

Now let it work. Mischief, thou art afoot,
Take thou what course thou wilt!
(with greater intensity, gesturing) Bring me
to Octavius.

Exit ANTONY *stage right.*

✱ **SCENE 6.** (ACT III, SCENE III)

A street.

Enter NARRATOR *from stage rear, coming downstage center.*

NARRATOR

Cinna the Poet meets the mob and discovers he has an unfortunate name.

Exit NARRATOR *stage left.*

Enter CINNA THE POET, *walking tentatively in from stage left.*

CINNA THE POET

I dreamt tonight that I did feast with Caesar,
And things unlucky charge my fantasy:
I have no will to wander forth of doors,
Yet something leads me forth.

Enter CITIZENS *from stage right, shouting and brandishing sticks, swords, and clubs.*

CITIZEN ONE

What is your name?

CITIZEN TWO

Whither are you going?

CITIZEN THREE

Where do you dwell?

CINNA THE POET

What is my name? Whither am I going? Where do I dwell? Briefly, I dwell by the Capitol.

CITIZEN THREE *(advancing one step stage left toward* CINNA THE POET*)*

Your name, sir, truly.

CINNA THE POET

Truly, my name is Cinna.

CINNA THE POET *retreats a step stage left.*

CITIZEN ONE

Tear him to pieces; he's a conspirator.

CINNA THE POET

I am Cinna the Poet, *(backing up one step)* *(more fervently)* I am Cinna the Poet.

He backs up another step.

CITIZEN FOUR

Tear him for his bad verses, tear him for his bad verses.

CINNA THE POET

I am not Cinna the conspirator.

He backs up against stage left pillar.

CITIZEN FOUR

It is no matter, his name's Cinna; pluck but his name out of his heart, and turn him going.

CITIZENS *descend on* CINNA THE POET, *surrounding him.*

CINNA THE POET *crumples to the ground and screams.*

SOUND OPERATOR *plays* Sound Cue #6 ("Drums and recorder").

CITIZEN THREE

Tear him, tear him! Come, brands ho! Fire-brands:
To Brutus's,

CITIZENS *(echoing)*

To Brutus's!

CITIZEN THREE

To Cassius's;

CITIZENS *(echoing)*

To Cassius's!

CITIZEN THREE

Burn all: some to Decius's house,

CITIZENS *(echoing)*

To Decius's!

CITIZEN THREE

And some to Casca's!

CITIZENS *(echoing)*

To Casca's!

CITIZEN THREE

Away, go!

Exit CITIZENS *stage right, yelling and brandishing their weapons.*

SOOTHSAYER *feels his way onstage. He moves toward* CINNA THE POET'S *body and touches him with his walking stick.* SOOTHSAYER *drops his stick and fumbles off stage left.*

✶ **SCENE 7.** (ACT IV, SCENE III)

BRUTUS'S *tent.*

Enter CHORUS *from stage right and stage left, coming to center stage. Their entrance blocks the body of* CINNA THE POET, *who exits stage rear.*

Enter NARRATOR *from stage left. She places a chair at center stage and walks downstage center.*

NARRATOR

Brutus and Cassius argue; Brutus informs Cassius that his wife, Portia, has killed herself. Brutus and Cassius plan to march to Philippi to challenge the armies of Antony and Octavius. Caesar's ghost invites himself along.

Exit NARRATOR *stage left.*

Enter BRUTUS *and* CASSIUS *from stage right.*

BRUTUS

I have here received letters,
That young Octavius and Mark Antony
Come down upon us with a mighty power,
Bending their expedition toward Philippi.
The enemy increaseth every day.

CHORUS *raise swords up.*

There is a tide in the affairs of men,
Which, taken at the flood, leads on to fortune.

CHORUS *hold swords forward.*

On such a full sea are we now afloat;
And we must take the current when it serves,
Or lose our ventures.

CHORUS *hold swords downward.*

CASSIUS

Then, with your will,
We'll meet them at Philippi.
Good night:
Early tomorrow will we rise, and hence.

Exit CASSIUS *stage left.*

Enter the GHOST OF CAESAR *from stage rear.*

CHORUS *(whispering in a wave, stage right to stage left)*
Brutus!

GHOST *moves through* CHORUS *toward* BRUTUS.

BRUTUS

Ha! Who comes here?
Art thou any thing?
Art thou some god, some angel, or some devil,
That makest my blood cold and my hair to stare?

GHOST

Thy evil spirit, Brutus.

CHORUS *(whispering, stage left to stage right)*
Brutus!

BRUTUS

Why comest thou?

GHOST

To tell thee thou shalt see me at Philippi.

CHORUS *(whispering)*

At Philippi.

BRUTUS

Why, I will see thee at Philippi, then.

Exit GHOST *stage right.*

Ill spirit, I would hold more talk with thee.

CHORUS *(whispering)*

Ill spirit.

Exit CHORUS *stage right.*

Exit BRUTUS *stage rear, striking chair.*

✷ **SCENE 8.** (ACT V, SCENE III)

The field of battle.

Enter NARRATOR *from stage rear, coming downstage center.*

NARRATOR

War rages on, and not all lives lost are on the battlefield.

Exit NARRATOR *stage left.*

SOUND OPERATOR *plays* Sound Cue #7 ("Drums").

Enter CASSIUS *and* PINDARUS *from stage right.*

CASSIUS

O, look, Pindarus, look, the villains fly!
Myself have to mine own turn'd enemy.

PINDARUS

O Cassius, Brutus gave the word too early;
We by Antony are all enclosed.

CASSIUS

Look, look, Pindarus;
Are those my tents where I perceive the fire?
O, coward that I am, to live so long,
To see my best friend ta'en before my face!
(to Pindarus)
Come hither, sirrah: and with this good sword,

That ran through Caesar's bowels, search this bosom.
Take thou the hilts; guide thou the sword.

PINDARUS *stabs* CASSIUS.

Caesar, thou art revenged,
Even with the sword that kill'd thee.

CASSIUS *dies.*

PINDARUS

So, I am free; O Cassius,
Far from this country Pindarus shall run.

Exit PINDARUS *stage right.*

Enter TITINIUS *and* MESSALA *from stage left.*

TITINIUS

Cassius is no more.
The sun of Rome is set! Our day is gone.

MESSALA

Mistrust of good success hath done this deed.

TITINIUS

Hie you, Messala,
And I will seek for Pindarus the while.

Exit MESSALA *stage left.*

Brave Cassius?
Alas, thou hast misconstrued every thing!
(crowns CASSIUS *with garland)*
By your leave, gods:—this is a Roman's part
Come, Cassius's sword, and find Titinius's heart.

TITINIUS *kills himself.*

SOUND OPERATOR *plays Sound Cue #8 ("Drums").*

Re-enter MESSALA *from stage left with* BRUTUS *and* STRATO. *They see the bodies of* CASSIUS *and* TITINIUS.

BRUTUS

O Julius Caesar, thou art mighty yet!
Thy spirit walks abroad and turns our swords
In our own proper entrails.

SOUND OPERATOR *plays* Sound Cue #9 ("Drums").

BRUTUS

Are yet two Romans living such as these?
The last of all the Romans, fare thee well!
Friends, I owe more tears
To this dead man than you shall see me pay.
Let us to the field. Set our battles on:
'Tis three o'clock; and, Romans, yet ere night
We shall try fortune in a second fight.

Exit ALL *stage right.*

✷ **SCENE 9** (ACT V, SCENE V)

Another part of the field.

Enter NARRATOR *from stage rear, coming downstage center.*

NARRATOR

Brutus dies by the same hand that killed his friend Caesar: his own. Antony praises Brutus as the only honorable conspirator.

Exit NARRATOR *stage left.*

Enter BRUTUS, CLITUS, STRATO, *and* VOLUMNIUS *from stage right.*

BRUTUS

Come, poor remains of friends, rest on this rock.
(whispering) Hark thee, Clitus.

CLITUS

What, I, my lord? No, not for all the world.
I'll rather kill myself.

BRUTUS *(to* VOLUMNIUS*)*

Come hither, good Volumnius; list a word.
The ghost of Caesar hath appear'd to me:
I know my hour is come.
Our enemies have beat us to the pit:

SOUND OPERATOR *plays* Sound Cue #10 ("Drums").

Good Volumnius, I prithee,
Hold thou my sword-hilts, whilst I run on it.

VOLUMNIUS

That's not an office for a friend, my lord.

SOUND OPERATOR *plays* Sound Cue #11 ("Drums").

BRUTUS

Farewell to you.
Countrymen,
My heart doth joy that yet in all my life
I found no man but he was true to me.
I shall have glory by this losing day.

SOUND OPERATOR *plays Sound Cue #12 ("Drums").*

ALL *(from offstage)*

Fly, fly!

CLITUS

Fly, my lord, fly.

BRUTUS

Hence! I will follow.

Exit CLITUS *and* VOLUMNIUS *stage left.*

I prithee, Strato, stay thou by thy lord:
Hold then my sword, and turn away thy face,
While I do run upon it. Wilt thou, Strato?

STRATO

Give me your hand first. Fare you well, my lord.

BRUTUS

Farewell, good Strato.

BRUTUS *runs into his own sword, held by* **STRATO.**

Caesar, now be still:
I kill'd not thee with half so good a will.

BRUTUS *dies.*

SOUND OPERATOR *plays Sound Cue #13 ("Drums").*

Enter **ANTONY** *and* **MESSALA** *from stage right.*

Enter **ALL** *as* **ANTONY** *begins speech.*

ANTONY

This was the noblest Roman of them all:

CONSPIRATORS

All the conspirators save only he
Did that they did in envy of great Caesar.

PORTIA AND CALPURNIA

He only, in a general honest thought
And common good to all, made one of them.

ALL *(with rising intensity)*

His life was gentle, and the elements
So mix'd in him that Nature might stand up
And say to all the world
(gesturing out to audience with arms)
'This was a man!'

ALL *hold hands and take a bow. Exeunt.*

* PERFORMING SHAKESPEARE

HOW *THE 30-MINUTE SHAKESPEARE* WAS BORN

In 1981 I performed a "Shakespeare Juggling" piece called "To Juggle or Not To Juggle" at the first Folger Library Secondary School Shakespeare Festival. The audience consisted of about 200 Washington, D.C. area high school students who had just performed thirty-minute versions of Shakespeare plays for each other and were jubilant over the experience. I was dressed in a jester's outfit, and my job was to entertain them. I juggled and jested and played with Shakespeare's words, notably Hamlet's "To be or not to be" soliloquy, to very enthusiastic response. I was struck by how much my "Shakespeare Juggling" resonated with a group who had just performed Shakespeare themselves. "Getting" Shakespeare is a heady feeling, especially for adolescents, and I am continually delighted at how much joy and satisfaction young people derive from performing Shakespeare. Simply reading and studying this great playwright does not even come close to inspiring the kind of enthusiasm that comes from performance.

Surprisingly, many of these students were not "actor types." A good percentage of the students performing Shakespeare that day were part of an English class which had rehearsed the plays during class time. Fifteen years later, when I first started directing plays in D.C. public schools as a Teaching Artist with the Folger Shakespeare Library, I entered a ninth grade English class as a guest and spent two or three days a week for two or three months preparing students for the Folger's annual Secondary School Shakespeare Festival. I have conducted this annual residency with the Folger ever since. Every year for seven action-packed days, eight groups of students between grades seven and twelve tread the boards onstage at the Folger's Elizabethan Theatre, a grand recreation of a sixteenth-century venue with a three-tiered gallery, carved oak columns, and a sky-painted canopy.

As noted on the Folger website (www.folger.edu), "The festival is a celebration of the Bard, not a competition. Festival commentators—drawn from the professional theater and Shakespeare education communities—recognize exceptional performances, student directors, and good spirit amongst the students with selected awards at the end of each day. They are also available to share feedback with the students."

My annual Folger Teaching Artist engagement, directing a Shakespeare play in a public high school English class, is the most challenging and the most rewarding thing I do all year. I hope this book can bring you the same rewards.

GETTING STARTED

GAMES

How can you get an English class (or any other group of young people, or even adults) to start the seemingly daunting task of performing a Shakespeare play? You have already successfully completed the critical first step, which is buying this book. You hold in your hand a performance-ready, thirty-minute cutting of a Shakespeare play, with stage directions to get the actors moving about the stage purposefully. But it's a good idea to warm the group up with some theater games.

One good initial exercise is called "Positive/Negative Salutations." Students stand in two lines facing each other (four or five students in each line) and, reading from index cards, greet each other, first with a "Positive" salutation in Shakespeare's language (using actual phrases from the plays), followed by a "negative" greeting.

Additionally, short vocal exercises are an essential part of the preparation process. The following is a very simple and effective vocal warm-up: Beginning with the number two, have the whole group count to twenty using increments of two (i.e., "Two, four, six . . ."). Increase the volume slightly with each number, reaching top volume with "twenty," and then decrease the volume while counting back down, so that the students are practically whispering when they arrive again at "two." This exercise teaches dynamics and allows them to get loud as a group without any individual pressure. Frequently during a rehearsal period, if a student is mumbling inaudibly, I will refer back to this exercise as a reminder that we can and often do belt it out!

"Stomping Words" is a game that is very helpful at getting a handle on Shakespeare's rhythm. Choose a passage in iambic pentameter and have the group members walk around the room in a circle, stomping their feet on the second beat of each line:

> Two **house**-holds, **both** a-**like** in **dig**-nity
> In **fair** Ve-**ro**na **Where** we **lay** our **scene**

Do the same thing with a prose passage, and have the students discuss their experience with it, including points at which there is an extra beat, etc., and what, if anything, it might signify.

I end every vocal warm-up with a group reading of one of the speeches from the play, emphasizing diction and projection, bouncing off consonants, and encouraging the group members to listen to each other so that they can speak the lines together in unison. For variety I will throw in some classic "tongue twisters" too, such as, "The sixth sheik's sixth sheep is sick."

The Folger Shakespeare Library's website (http://www.folger.edu) and their book series *Shakespeare Set Free,* edited by Peggy O'Brien, are two great resources for getting started with a performance-based teaching of Shakespeare in the classroom. The Folger website has numerous helpful resources and activities, many submitted by teachers, for helping a class actively participate in the process of getting to know a Shakespeare play. For more simple theater games, Viola Spolin's *Theatre Games for the Classroom* is very helpful, as is one I use frequently, *Theatre Games for Young Performers.*

HATS AND PROPS

Introducing a few hats and props early in the process is a good way to get the action going. Hats, in particular, provide a nice avenue for giving young actors a non-verbal way of getting into character. In the opening weeks, when students are still holding onto their scripts, a hat can give an actor a way to "feel" like a character. Young actors are natural masters at injecting their own personality into what they wear, and even small choices made with how a hat is worn (jauntily, shadily, cockily, mysteriously) provide a starting point for discussion of specific characters, their traits, and their relationships with other characters. All such discussions always lead back to one thing: the text. "Mining the text" is consistently the best strategy for uncovering the mystery of Shakespeare's language. That is where all the answers lie: in the words themselves.

WHAT DO THE WORDS MEAN?

It is essential that young actors know what they are saying when they recite Shakespeare. If not, they might as well be scat singing, riffing on sounds and rhythm but not conveying a specific meaning. The real question is: What do the words mean? The answer is multifaceted, and can be found in more than one place. The New Folger Library paperback editions of the plays themselves (edited by Barbara Mowat and Paul Werstine, Washington Square Press) are a great resource for understanding Shakespeare's words and passages and "translating" them into modern English. These editions also contain chapters on Shakespeare's language, his life, his theater, a "Modern Perspective," and further reading. There is a wealth of scholarship embedded in these wonderful books, and I make it a point to read them cover to cover before embarking on a play-directing project. At the very least, it is a good idea for any adult who intends to direct a Shakespeare play with a group of students to go through the explanatory notes that appear on the pages facing the text. These explanatory notes are an indispensable "translation tool."

The best way to get students to understand what Shakespeare's words mean is to ask them what they think they mean. Students have their own associations with the words and with how they sound and feel. The best ideas on how to perform Shakespeare often come directly from the students, not from anybody else's notion. If a student has an idea or feeling about a word or passage, and it resonates with her emotionally, physically, or spiritually, then Shakespeare's words can be a vehicle for her feelings. That can result in some powerful performances!

I make it my job as director to read the explanatory notes in the Folger text, but I make it clear to the students that almost "anything goes" when trying to understand Shakespeare. There are no wrong interpretations. Students have their own experiences, with some shared and some uniquely their own. If someone has an association with the phrase "canker-blossom," or if the words make that student or his character feel or act a certain way, then that is the "right" way to decipher it.

I encourage the students to refer to the Folger text's explanatory notes and to keep a pocket dictionary handy. Young actors must attach some meaning to every word or line they recite. If I feel an actor is glossing over a word, I will stop him and ask him what he is saying. If he doesn't know, we will figure it out together as a group.

PROCESS VS. PRODUCT

The process of learning Shakespeare by performing one of his plays is more important than whether everybody remembers his lines or whether somebody misses a cue or an entrance. But my Teaching Artist residencies have always had the end goal of a public performance for about 200 other students, so naturally the performance starts to take precedence over the process somewhere around dress rehearsal in the students' minds. It is my job to make sure the actors are prepared—otherwise they will remember the embarrassing moment of a public mistake and not the glorious triumph of owning a Shakespeare play.

In one of my earlier years of play directing, I was sitting in the audience as one of my narrators stood frozen on stage for at least a minute, trying to remember her opening line. I started scrambling in my backpack below my seat for a script, at last prompting her from the audience. Despite her fine performance, that embarrassing moment is all she remembered from the whole experience. Since then I have made sure to assign at least one person to prompt from backstage if necessary. Additionally, I inform the entire cast that if somebody is dying alone out there, it is okay to rescue him or her with an offstage prompt.

There is always a certain amount of stage fright that will accompany a performance, especially a public one for an unfamiliar audience. As a director, I live with stage fright as well, even though I am not appearing on stage. The only antidote to this is work and preparation. If a young actor is struggling with her lines, I make sure to arrange for a session where we run lines over the telephone. I try to set up a buddy system so that students can run lines with their peers, and this often works well. But if somebody does not have a "buddy," I will personally make the time to help out myself. As I assure my students from the outset, I am not going to let them fail or embarrass themselves. They need an experienced leader. And if the leader has experience in teaching but not in directing Shakespeare, then he needs this book!

It is a good idea to culminate in a public performance, as opposed to an in-class project, even if it is only for another classroom. Student actors want to show their newfound Shakespearian thespian skills to an outside group, and this goal motivates them to do a good job. In that respect, "product" is important. Another wonderful bonus to performing a play is that it is a unifying group effort. Students learn teamwork. They learn to give focus to another actor when he is speaking, and to play off of other characters. I like to end each performance with the entire cast reciting a passage in unison. This is a powerful ending, one that reaffirms the unity of the group.

SEEING SHAKESPEARE PERFORMED

It is very helpful for young actors to see Shakespeare performed by a group of professionals, whether they are appearing live on stage (preferable but not always possible) or on film. Because an entire play can take up two or more full class periods, time may be an issue. I am fortunate because thanks to a local foundation that underwrites theater education in the schools, I have been able to take my school groups to a Folger Theatre matinee of the play that they are performing. I always pick a play that is being performed locally that season. But not all group leaders are that lucky. Fortunately, there is the Internet, specifically YouTube. A quick YouTube search for "Shakespeare" can unearth thousands of results, many appropriate for the classroom.

The first "Hamlet" result showed an 18-year-old African-American actor on the streets of Camden, New Jersey, delivering a riveting performance of Hamlet's "The play's the thing." The second clip was from *Cat Head Theatre,* an animation of cats performing Hamlet. Of course, YouTube boasts not just alley cats and feline thespians, but also clips by true legends of the stage, such as John Gielgud and Richard Burton. These clips can be saved and shown in classrooms, providing useful inspiration.

One advantage of the amazing variety of clips available on YouTube is that students can witness the wide range of interpretations for any given scene, speech, or character in Shakespeare, thus freeing them from any preconceived notion that there is a "right" way to do it. Furthermore, modern interpretations of the Bard may appeal to those who are put off by the "thees and thous" of Elizabethan speech.

By seeing Shakespeare performed either live or on film, students are able to hear the cadence, rhythm, vocal dynamics, and pronunciation of the language, and they can appreciate the life that other actors breathe into the characters. They get to see the story told dramatically, which inspires them to tell their own version.

PUTTING IT ALL TOGETHER

THE STEPS

After a few sessions of theater games to warm up the group, it's time to begin the process of casting the play. Each play cutting in *The 30-Minute Shakespeare* series includes a cast list and a sample program, demonstrating which parts have been divided. Cast size is generally between twelve and thirty students, with major roles frequently assigned to more than one performer. In other words, one student may play Juliet in the first scene, another in the second scene, and yet another in the third. This will distribute the parts evenly so that there is no "star of the show." Furthermore, this prevents actors from being burdened with too many lines. If I have an actor who is particularly talented or enthusiastic, I will give her a bigger role. It is important to go with the grain—one cast member's enthusiasm can be contagious.

I provide the performer of each shared role with a similar headpiece and/or cape, so that the audience can keep track of the characters. When there are sets of twins, I try to use blue shirts and red shirts, so that the audience has at least a fighting chance of figuring it out! Other than these costume consistencies, I rely on the text and the audience's observance to sort out the doubling of characters. Generally, the audience can follow because we are telling the story.

Some participants are shy and do not wish to speak at all on stage. To these students I assign non-speaking parts and technical roles such as sound operator and stage manager. However, I always get everybody on stage at some point, even if it is just for the final group speech, because I want every group member to experience what it is like to be on a stage as part of an ensemble.

CASTING THE PLAY

Young people can be self-conscious and nervous with "formal" auditions, especially if they have little or no acting experience.

I conduct what I call an "informal" audition process. I hand out a questionnaire asking students if there is any particular role that they desire, whether they play a musical instrument. To get a feel for them as people, I also ask them to list one or two hobbies or interests. Occasionally this will inform my casting decisions. If someone can juggle, and the play has the part of a Fool, that skill may come in handy. Dancing or martial arts abilities can also be applied to roles.

For the auditions, I do not use the cut script. I have students stand and read from the Folger edition of the complete text in order to hear how they fare with the longer passages. I encourage them to breathe and carry their vocal energy all the way to the end of a long line of text. I also urge them to play with diction, projection, modulation, and dynamics, elements of speech that we have worked on in our vocal warm-ups and theater games.

I base my casting choices largely on reading ability, vocal strength, and enthusiasm for the project. If someone has requested a particular role, I try to honor that request. I explain that even with a small part, an actor can create a vivid character that adds a lot to the play. Wide variations in personality types can be utilized: if there are two students cast as Romeo, one brooding and one effusive, I try to put the more brooding Romeo in an early lovelorn scene, and place the effusive Romeo in the balcony scene. Occasionally one gets lucky, and the doubling of characters provides a way to match personality types with different aspects of a character's personality. But also be aware of the potential serendipity of non-traditional casting. For example, I have had one of the smallest students in the class play a powerful Othello. True power comes from within!

Generally, I have more females than males in a class, so women are more likely (and more willing) to play male characters than vice versa.

Rare is the high school boy who is brave enough to play a female character, which is unfortunate because it can reap hilarious results.

GET OUTSIDE HELP

Every time there is a fight scene in one of the plays I am directing, I call on my friend Michael Tolaydo, a professional actor and theater professor at St. Mary's College, who is an expert in all aspects of theater, including fight choreography. Not only does Michael stage the fight, but he does so in a way that furthers the action of the play, highlighting character's traits and bringing out the best in the student actors. Fight choreography must be done by an expert or somebody could get hurt. In the absence of such help, super slow-motion fights are always a safe bet and can be quite effective, especially when accompanied by a soundtrack on the boom box.

During dress rehearsals I invite my friend Hilary Kacser. a Washington-area actor and dialect coach for two decades. Because I bring her in late in the rehearsal process, I have her direct her comments to me, which I then filter and relay to the cast. This avoids confusing the cast with a second set of directions. This caveat only applies to general directorial comments from outside visitors. Comments on specific artistic disciplines such as dance, music, and stage combat can come from the outside experts themselves.

If you work in a school, you might have helpful resources within your own building, such as a music or dance teacher who could contribute their expertise to a scene. If nobody is available in your school, try seeking out a member of the local professional theater. Many local performing artists will be glad to help, and the students are usually thrilled to have a visit from a professional performer.

LET STUDENTS BRING THEMSELVES INTO THE PLAY

The best ideas often come from the students themselves. If a young actor has a notion of how to play a scene, I will always give that idea a try. In a rehearsal of *Henry IV, Part 1,* one traveler jumped into the other's arms when they were robbed. It got a huge laugh. This was something that they did on instinct. We kept that bit for the performance, and it worked wonderfully.

As a director, you have to foster an environment in which that kind of spontaneity can occur. The students have to feel safe to experiment. In the same production of *Henry IV,* Falstaff and Hal invented a little fist bump "secret handshake" to use in the battle scene. The students were having fun and bringing parts of themselves into the play. Shakespeare himself would have approved. When possible I try to err on the side of fun because if the young actors are having fun, then they will commit themselves to the project. The beauty of the language, the story, the characters, and the pathos will follow.

There is a balance to be achieved here, however. In that same production of *Henry IV, Part 1,* the student who played Bardolph was having a great time with her character. She carried a leather wineskin around and offered it up to the other characters in the tavern. It was a prop with which she developed a comic relationship. At the end of our thirty-minute *Henry IV, Part 1,* I added a scene from *Henry IV, Part 2* as a coda: The new King Henry V (formerly Falstaff's drinking and carousing buddy Hal) rejects Falstaff, banishing him from within ten miles of the King. It is a sad and sobering moment, one of the most powerful in the play.

But at the performance, in the middle of the King's rejection speech (played by a female student, and her only speech), Bardolph offered her flask to King Henry and got a big laugh, thus not only upstaging the King but also undermining the seriousness and poignancy of the whole scene. She did not know any better; she was bringing herself to the character as I had been encouraging her to do. But it was inappropriate, and in subsequent seasons, if I foresaw something like that happening as an individual joyfully occupied a character, I attempted to prevent it. Some things we cannot predict. Now I make sure to issue a statement warning against changing any of the blocking on show day, and to watch out for upstaging one's peers.

FOUR FORMS OF ENGAGEMENT: VOCAL, EMOTIONAL, PHYSICAL, AND INTELLECTUAL

When directing a Shakespeare play with a group of students, I always start with the words themselves because the words have the power to engage the emotions, mind, and body. Also, I start with the words in action, as in the previously mentioned exercise, "Positive and Negative Salutations." Students become physically engaged; their bodies react to the images the words evoke. The words have the power to trigger a switch in both the teller and the listener, eliciting both an emotional and physical reaction. I have never heard a student utter the line "Fie! Fie! You counterfeit, you puppet you!" without seeing him change before my eyes. His spine stiffens, his eyes widen, and his fingers point menacingly.

Having used Shakespeare's words to engage the students emotionally and physically, one can then return to the text for a more reflective discussion of what the words mean to us personally. I always make sure to leave at least a few class periods open for discussion of the text, line by line, to ensure that students understand intellectually what they feel viscerally. The advantage to a performance-based teaching of Shakespeare is that by engaging students vocally, emotionally, and physically, it is then much easier to engage them intellectually because they are invested in the words, the characters, and the story. We always start on our feet, and later we sit and talk.

SIX ELEMENTS OF DRAMA: PLOT, CHARACTER, THEME, DICTION, MUSIC, AND SPECTACLE

Over two thousand years ago, Aristotle's *Poetics* outlined six elements of drama, in order of importance: Plot, Character, Theme, Diction, Music, and Spectacle. Because Shakespeare was foremost a playwright, it is helpful to take a brief look at these six elements as they relate to directing a Shakespeare play in the classroom.

PLOT (ACTION)

To Aristotle, plot was the most important element. One of the purposes of *The 30-Minute Shakespeare* is to provide a script that tells Shakespeare's stories, as opposed to concentrating on one scene. In a thirty-minute edit of a Shakespeare play, some plot elements are necessarily omitted. For the sake of a full understanding of the characters' relationships and motivations, it is helpful to make short plot summaries of each scene so that students are aware of their characters' arcs throughout the play. The scene descriptions in the Folger editions are sufficient to fill in the plot holes. Students can read the descriptions aloud during class time to ensure that the story is clear and that no plot elements are neglected. Additionally, there are one-page charts in the Folger editions of *Shakespeare Set Free,* indicating characters' relations graphically, with lines connecting families and factions to give students a visual representation of what can often be complex interrelationships, particularly in Shakespeare's history plays.

Young actors love action. That is why *The 30-Minute Shakespeare* includes dynamic blocking (stage direction) that allows students to tell the story in a physically dramatic fashion. Characters' movements on the stage are always motivated by the text itself.

CHARACTER

I consider myself a facilitator and a director more than an acting teacher. I want the students' understanding of their characters to spring from the text and the story. From there, I encourage them to consider how their character might talk, walk, stand, sit, eat, and drink. I also urge students to consider characters' motivations, objectives, and relationships, and I will ask pointed questions to that end during the rehearsal process. I try not to show the students how I would perform a scene, but if no ideas are forthcoming from anybody in the class, I will suggest a minimum of two possibilities for how the character might respond.

At times students may want more guidance and examples. Over thirteen years of directing plays in the classroom, I have wavered between wanting all the ideas to come from the students, and deciding that I need to be more of a "director," telling them what I would like to see them doing. It is a fine line, but in recent years I have decided that if I don't see enough dynamic action or characterization, I will step in and "direct" more. But I always make sure to leave room for students to bring themselves into the characters because their own ideas are invariably the best.

THEME (THOUGHTS, IDEAS)

In a typical English classroom, theme will be a big topic for discussion of a Shakespeare play. Using a performance-based method of teaching Shakespeare, an understanding of the play's themes develops from "mining the text" and exploring Shakespeare's words and his story. If the students understand what they are saying and how that relates to their characters and the overall story, the plays' themes will emerge clearly. We always return to the text itself. There are a number of elegant computer programs, such as www.wordle.net, that will count the number of recurring words in a passage and illustrate them graphically. For example, if the word "jealousy" comes up more than any other word in *Othello,* it will appear in a larger font. Seeing the words displayed by size in this way can offer up illuminating insights into the interaction between words in the text and the play's themes. Your computer-minded students might enjoy searching for such tidbits. There are more internet tools and websites in the Additional Resources section at the back of this book.

I cannot overstress the importance of acting out the play in understanding its themes. By embodying the roles of Othello and Iago and reciting their words, students do not simply comprehend the themes intellectually, but understand them kinesthetically, physically, and emotionally. They are essentially *living* the characters' jealousy, pride, and feelings about race. The themes of appearance vs.

reality, good vs. evil, honesty, misrepresentation, and self-knowledge (or lack thereof) become physically felt as well as intellectually understood. Performing Shakespeare delivers a richer understanding than that which comes from just reading the play. Students can now relate the characters' conflicts to their own struggles.

DICTION (LANGUAGE)

If I had to cite one thing I would like my actors to take from their experience of performing a play by William Shakespeare, it is an appreciation and understanding of the beauty of Shakespeare's language. The language is where it all begins and ends. Shakespeare's stories are dramatic, his characters are rich and complex, and his settings are exotic and fascinating, but it is through his language that these all achieve their richness. This leads me to spend more time on language than on any other element of the performance.

Starting with daily vocal warm-ups, many of them using parts of the script or other Shakespearean passages, I consistently emphasize the importance of the words. Young actors often lack experience in speaking clearly and projecting their voices outward, so in addition to comprehension, I emphasize projection, diction, breathing, pacing, dynamics, coloring of words, and vocal energy. *Theatre Games for Young Performers* contains many effective vocal exercises, as does the Folger's *Shakespeare Set Free* series. Consistent emphasis on all aspects of Shakespeare's language, especially on how to speak it effectively, is the most important element to any Shakespeare performance with a young cast.

MUSIC

A little music can go a long way in setting a mood for a thirty-minute Shakespeare play. I usually open the show with a short passage of music to set the tone. Thirty seconds of music played on a boom box operated by a student can provide a nice introduction to the play, create an atmosphere for the audience, and give the actors a sense of place and feeling.

iTunes is a good starting point for choosing your music. Typing in "Shakespeare" or "Hamlet" or "jealousy" (if you are going for a theme) will result in an excellent selection of aural performance enhancers at the very reasonable price of ninety-nine cents each (or free of charge, see Additional Resources section). Likewise, fight sounds, foreboding sounds, weather sounds (rain, thunder), trumpet sounds, etc. are all readily available online at affordable cost. I typically include three sound cues in a play, just enough to enhance but not overpower a production. The boom box operator sits on the far right or left of the stage, not backstage, so he can see the action. This also has the added benefit of having somebody out there with a script, capable of prompting in a pinch.

SPECTACLE

Aristotle considered spectacle the least important aspect of drama. Students tend to be surprised at this since we are used to being bombarded with production values on TV and video, often at the expense of substance. In my early days of putting on student productions, I would find myself hamstrung by my own ambitions in the realm of scenic design.

A simple bench or two chairs set on the stage are sufficient. The sense of "place" can be achieved through language and acting. Simple set dressing, a few key props, and some tasteful, emblematic costume pieces will go a long way toward providing all the "spectacle" you need.

In the stage directions to the plays in *The 30-Minute Shakespeare* series, I make frequent use of two large pillars stage left and right at the Folger Shakespeare Library's Elizabethan Theatre. I also have characters frequently entering and exiting from "stage rear." Your stage will have a different layout. Take a good look at the performing space you will be using and see if there are any elements that can be incorporated into your own stage directions. Is there a balcony? Can characters enter from the audience? (Make sure that they can get there from backstage, unless you want them waiting in the lobby until their entrance, which may be impractical.) If possible, make sure to rehearse in that space a few times to fix any technical issues and perhaps discover a few fun staging variations that will add pizzazz and dynamics to your own show.

The real spectacle is in the telling of the tale. Wooden swords are handy for characters that need them. Students should be warned at the outset that playing with swords outside of the scene is verboten. Letters, moneybags, and handkerchiefs should all have plentiful duplicates kept in a small prop box, as well as with a stage manager, because they tend to disappear in the hands of adolescents. After every rehearsal and performance, I recommend you personally sweep the rehearsal or performance area immediately for stray props. It is amazing what gets left behind.

Ultimately, the performances are about language and human drama, not set pieces, props, and special effects. Fake blood, glitter, glass, and liquids have no place on the stage; they are a recipe for disaster, or, at the very least, a big mess. On the other hand, the props that are employed can often be used effectively to convey character, as in Bardolph's aforementioned relationship with his wineskin.

PITFALLS AND SOLUTIONS

Putting on a play in a high school classroom is not easy. There are problems with enthusiasm, attitude, attention, and line memorization, to name a few. As anybody who has directed a play will tell you, it is always darkest before the dawn. My experience is that after one or two days of utter despair just before the play goes up, show day breaks and the play miraculously shines. To quote a recurring gag in one of my favorite movies, *Shakespeare in Love:* "It's a mystery."

ENTHUSIASM, FRUSTRATION, AND DISCIPLINE

Bring the enthusiasm yourself. Feed on the energy of the eager students, and others will pick up on that. Keep focused on the task at hand. Arrive prepared. Enthusiasm comes as you make headway. Ultimately, it helps to remind the students that a play is fun. I try to focus on the positive attributes of the students, rather than the ones that drive me crazy. This is easier said than done, but it is important. One season, I yelled at the group two days in a row. On day two of yelling, they tuned me out, and it took me a while to win them back. I learned my lesson; since then I've tried not to raise my voice out of anger or frustration. As I grow older and more mature, it is important for me to lead by example. It has been years since I yelled at a student group. If I am disappointed in their work or their behavior, I will express my disenchantment in words, speaking from the heart as somebody who cares about them and cares about our performance and our experience together. I find that fundamentally, young people want to please, to do well, and to be liked. If there is a serious discipline problem, I will hand it over to the regular classroom teacher, the administrator, or the parent.

LINE MEMORIZATION

Students may have a hard time memorizing lines. In these cases, see if you can pair them up with a "buddy" and existing friend who will run lines with them in person or over the phone after school. If students do not have such a "buddy," I volunteer to run lines with them myself. If serious line memorization problems arise that cannot be solved through work, then two students can switch parts if it is early enough in the rehearsal process. For doubled roles, the scene with fewer lines can go to the actor who is having memorization problems. Additionally, a few passages or lines can be cut. Again, it is important to address these issues early. Later cuts become more problematic as other actors have already memorized their cues. I have had to do late cuts about twice in thirteen years. While they have gotten us out of jams, it is best to assess early whether a student will have line memorization problems, and deal with the problem sooner rather than later.

In production, always keep several copies of the script backstage, as well as cheat sheets indicating cues, entrances, and scene changes. Make a prop list, indicating props for each scene, as well as props that are the responsibility of individual actors. Direct the Stage Manager and an Assistant Stage Manager to keep track of these items, and on show days, personally double-check if you can.

In thirteen years of preparing an inner-city public high school English class for a public performance on a field trip to the Folger Secondary School Shakespeare Festival, my groups and I have been beset by illness, emotional turmoil, discipline problems, stage fright, adolescent angst, midlife crises (not theirs), and all manner of other emergencies, including acts of God and nature. Despite the difficulties and challenges inherent in putting on a Shakespeare play with a group of young people, one amazing fact stands out in my experience. Here is how many times a student has been absent for show day: Zero. Somehow, everybody has always made it to the show, and the show has gone on. How can this be? It's a mystery.

✱ PERFORMANCE NOTES: *JULIUS CAESAR*

I directed this performance of *Julius Caesar* in 2012 with a group of high school seniors. These notes are the result of my own review of the performance video. They are not intended to be the "definitive" performance notes for all productions of *Julius Caesar.* Your production will be unique to you and your cast. That is the magic of live theater. What is interesting about these notes is that many of the performance details I mention were not part of the original stage directions. They either emerged spontaneously on performance day or were developed by students in rehearsal after the stage directions had been written into the script. Some of these pieces of stage business might work like a charm. Others may fall flat. My favorites are the ones that arise directly from the students themselves and demonstrate a union between actor and character, as if that individual has become a vehicle for the character he is playing. To witness an eighteen-year-old young man "become" Marc Antony as Shakespeare's words leave his mouth is a memorable moment indeed.

Most notable about this particular production was that I used a Chorus for the first time. This allowed for a greater overall participation level from all students and contributed greatly to the overall feel of the performance as an ensemble production. The Chorus provided visual and sound effects, verbal commentary, and emotional reactions to the action on the stage, which not only helped clarify the story, but also added to its power.

SCENE 1 (ACT I, SCENE II)

In this first scene of our 2012 production of *Julius Caesar*, the actor playing the Soothsayer ended up as Narrator One by coincidence, which led to an interesting piece of business. As the Narrator finished the line "An ill wind blows," members of the Chorus waved their hands in front of them to indicate wind, while the sound operator made recorder whistle and drum sounds. These actions transformed the actor from Narrator into the blind Soothsayer as she stumbled offstage holding her cane out in front of her.

We had originally planned to have a different actor in the role of the Soothsayer, but because she preferred the relative anonymity of the Chorus, we replaced her with the student who was already playing Narrator in Scene One. This is an example of how small staging changes can lead to new ideas. As staged, Narrator One began the scene in her Soothsayer costume, so having the Chorus "transform" her from Narrator into Soothsayer fulfilled a dual purpose: it provided a transition between the two personae and also set an ominous tone for the next few scenes, in which foul weather portends dark deeds.

The Chorus provides an additional sound effect early on in the scene: the flourish. As Caesar enters, all members of the Chorus raise their arms up and hum a "trumpet flourish" as if playing the instrument to herald his arrival. Live music, even in the absence of real musical instruments, imparts a feeling that pre-recorded sounds cannot. Not only does it engage the actors, but it has an immediacy and power all its own. Whenever possible, enlist the actors to provide live sound effects.

Note that when on stage, the Chorus is divided into two parts: Stage Right and Stage Left Chorus. The two sides form a "V" shape, which allows for better visibility and mirroring of each other's movements. (See Appendix for more information.)

Coincidence led to an unusual character pairing in the 2012 production. The actor playing Cinna the Poet also played a Chorus member in Scene One. Once the Soothsayer had been rendered "blind" at the play's opening, we needed somebody to help her off the stage. The actor playing Cinna volunteered, and we had her accompany the Soothsayer in her next appearance as well. We also chose for the Soothsayer to discover the terrible scene of Cinna's death near the end of the play. Thus, a relationship that was not in the text emerged out of the staging and added new depth to our production.

SCENE 2 (ACT II, SCENE I)

Narrator Two's final line, "Storm clouds gather," echoes Narrator One's "An ill wind blows," providing the Chorus with another opportunity to repeat the arm-waving wind depiction from Scene One. As the recorder and drum sounds play, the Chorus and sound operator's sonic and physical repetitions provide a non-verbal pallet against which the words and actions unfold.

Scene Two offers more opportunities for the Chorus to illustrate the text; they do so here by creating moving tableaux that illustrate specific phrases. On "think of him as a serpent's egg, which hatch'd would . . . kill him in the shell," I asked the Chorus members to suggest some moves for this line, and one student did such an artful job of physically depicting the text that I assigned her the role of Chorus Captain.

Our Chorus Captain snaked her arm up on "a serpents' egg, which hatch'd" and then brought it down swiftly to her midsection as if to stab herself on "would . . . kill him in the shell," simultaneously bending at the waist and lowering her head as if dying. To enhance this effect, the sound operator played a small shaker to suggest the hissing of a snake. It is amazing how much small details like this can add to a scene's mood and visual palette. (It is wise, however, not to overdo the sound cues. As with scene changes and set pieces, they should be used sparingly; if the production becomes overly complex, the stage crew and actors will be distracted from the more pressing business of tale telling.)

Recalling an incident from a staging of *Macbeth* several years prior, when an actor simply refused to go on with the scene until she heard a "shrieking owl," I had impressed upon the *Julius Caesar* cast the importance of continuing on in the absence of a sound cue. In this case, the sound operator was to hit a musical triangle three times to indicate chiming prior to the line "the clock hath stricken three." When he neglected to hit the triangle at the proper point, there was only a brief pause, and the actor portraying Cassius wisely proceeded with her line. Always remind your cast that in the face of miscues, absent sound effects, or any other stage mishaps: *keep going*. In fact, I would have preferred that the conspirators cock their heads as if listening to the chiming of a clock, but I was satisfied that they continued and did not let a flubbed sound cue derail the scene.

The second half of this scene features dialogue between Brutus and Portia that nicely illustrates their relationship. It is a dance of approach and avoidance, based on the predominant sentiment of each phrase being spoken. Portia moves toward Brutus on "Make me acquainted with your cause of grief," and Brutus moves away from Portia on "I am not well in health and that is all." Ask your actors to explore the couple's relationship by examining the text and finding words, phrases, and moments that can be enhanced by a movement, gesture, facial expression, or vocal inflection.

While the actor playing Portia wanted to turn her back fully on Brutus (and the audience) on the line "If it be no more, Portia is Brutus's harlot, not his wife," I encouraged her to speak and *then* turn, since to do so simultaneously would muffle her words. She forgot this note during performance, turning her back to the audience while saying the line, which greatly lessened its effect. This kind of staging error can easily be remedied for subsequent performances. In our case, we only had one performance of the play and were unable to fix it for later. That's showbiz.

Encourage actors to explore the richness and variety inherent in every acting and staging choice. Always come back to the text itself for clues. Portia uses the words "ungently," "sick," "once-commended," "heavy," and "harlot." Each of these words has an emotional connotation that can be enhanced physically or verbally. Once actors have explored both the meaning and feeling of the words, they can make choices that make the characters their own.

SCENE 3 (ACT II, SCENE II)

The Narrator for this scene seized her opening moment and made it her own. As she strode confidently and joyously onto the stage, she added a conversational intro of "Well, well, well" to her comic narration, accenting it with winks and hands-on-hips sassiness. It was the very embodiment of embracing a small role with utmost gusto, and she later won an acting award for her part. This young performer brought to the stage a joy and enthusiasm that cannot be taught, but it can be nurtured, encouraged, and applauded—and indeed it garnered extended laughter and applause from the appreciative audience.

I wanted Calpurnia's fear in Scene Three to be visceral, so I encouraged the actor and the Chorus echoing her to explore more primal screaming on the lines "Murder!" and "Caesar!" One very simple way to accomplish this in your production is to conduct the following rehearsal exercise: have your cast begin by saying the two words at a soft volume, and then have them increase the volume incrementally over ten repetitions until they are screaming. From there, they should repeat the lines at volume ten, gradually bringing them back down to a volume of one. This uncomplicated exercise in dynamics can be applied to any situation where you feel that a scene is lacking in vocal energy, urgency, or volume.

This technique contributed to the Chorus's piercing shriek after Calpurnia's line "and ghosts did shriek and squeal about the streets." The sheer intensity of their shriek gave Calpurnia something to react to. She jumped back, startled, and exclaimed, "And I do fear them." Whenever possible, give actors something to react to by encouraging them to move and speak with intensity and purpose. Acting is reacting.

There are several moments in this scene where the Chorus provides tableaux, either a mobile tableau to accompany smaller phrases or a fixed tableau to illustrate a larger passage. The tableau is an effective snapshot for helping audiences understand the scene, and it nudges actors to look deeper into the text, knowing that they have to provide a stage picture to represent it. Your cast can develop a physical vocabulary for this by participating in theater games in early rehearsals; choose small groups of four or five actors to present tableaux that illustrate portions of text.

SCENE 4 (ACT III, SCENE I)

In this critical scene, Caesar is murdered. Scenes containing stage combat, killings, or any sort of swordplay require a respect for the dangers inherent therein. Actors should be taught not to play with the weapons or use them outside of specific rehearsals, even if the swords are wooden or plastic. Because young actors tend to fidget with swords and daggers and wave them about randomly, I avoid using them as simple costume pieces and save them for their intended uses: fighting and killing. I have been fortunate to enlist my colleague, professional actor Michael Tolaydo, to stage fights in several of my productions, but a professional is not always available. A very effective technique for safely staging these fight and murder scenes is *slow motion*.

While the sound operator plays drum and recorder (drums on the approach, recorder on the stabbing), the conspirators kill Caesar in slow motion one by one. In this way, the sound of the recorder becomes associated with death. In rehearsal, I encouraged the actors playing the conspirators to think of a word or short phrase to say out loud while murdering Caesar (e.g., "I envy you!", "I do this for Rome!", "I do this because others do it!"). This helps ground the act of killing Caesar in a concrete and personal reason for each actor/character. In performance the actors did not cry out these phrases, but they had internalized them enough to add motivation and purpose to their actions. During the stabbing of Caesar, the sound effects of drums and recorder should intensify to create a powerful moment.

I impressed upon the actors the importance of providing the necessary ingredients to stir the audience to an emotional reaction.

Live sound effects have a great advantage over pre-recorded sounds: they can be played with passion. I asked the cast to imagine what it would feel like to kill somebody. Coupled with the aforementioned personal phrases for each conspirator, the killing of Caesar became not just a dramatic theatrical moment, but also an emotionally powerful one.

Before Brutus finally stabs Caesar, there should be a few seconds where the two look into each other's eyes. In our production, this moment was lost amidst the rush and stage commotion of the live performance. Crowd scenes, fight scenes, and killing scenes are tricky to stage, as they easily gain speed. The next time I want a still moment to take place in the midst of a chaotic scene, I will make a greater effort to emphasize its importance and rehearse it with a beat, such as actors counting "one, two, three" internally before continuing with the action.

Antony's monologue at the end of the scene, delivered while kneeling over Caesar's body, should also build in intensity. It should begin with tenderness and sorrow and then change to vengeance and anger. The actor playing Antony conveyed these dynamics well, and when he reached the line "Cry 'Havoc,' and let slip the dogs of war," he turned straight to the audience, his face full of the feelings the speech evoked, his voice strong and emotionally resonant, his eyes fiery. Sitting in the audience, I felt a chill. As a director, I can't always control when and where these powerful moments will occur; I can only try to provide the actors with the understanding and tools to bring about such a compelling instant themselves.

SCENE 5 (ACT III, SCENE II)

If a tragedy does not have any moments of outright comic relief, I try to provide one or two in the narration or staging. In this scene, I inserted the line "Politicians and their speeches: some things never change" at the end of the Narrator's speech. Narrator lines are an apt place for comic relief because, since we are between episodes, one does not risk undercutting the emotion of the scene. Shakespeare of course inserted bits of comic relief into many of his tragedies, but if the cutting or the play itself lacks laugh lines, then we can create them ourselves. Audiences need a moment of release before they dive back into the deep end of a Shakespearean tragedy.

The two speeches by Brutus and Antony in this scene rely on the Chorus to give them their proper context. The Chorus should begin the scene by agreeing with Brutus and end the scene by agreeing with Antony. How we get there and what emotional dynamics the crowd displays are what give the scene its power. The speeches themselves are compelling, but without crowd response they lack power. The power lies in the crowd and in our case, the Chorus.

As I did with the Conspirators in Caesar's murder scene, I encouraged each individual Chorus member to create a short "back story" to help with reactions to the speeches. Were they a person who tried to sway his neighbor or one who was swayed *by* his neighbor? What was their response to Caesar's murder? Joy at the killing of one they saw as a tyrant? Fear at the uncertainty that Caesar's death brought? By having each chorus member formulate an individual opinion and emotional response to the speeches, the audience can see how disparate individual feelings congeal into one crowd "group mind" by the end of the scene. Spurred by Antony's brilliant orating skills and influenced by their peers, Chorus members come together as an angry mob by the end of the scene.

The turning point in the scene comes when Antony kneels down and demonstrates the cuts in Caesar's mantle. At this point the Chorus members' disparate emotions merge into a group emotion of sadness, which by the end of the speech has transformed into anger. Our Chorus leader, in particular, stepped up to the challenge of responding as an individual to Antony's speech. She nodded or shook her head, looked at her neighbors as if to assess their responses, touched her heart. Others in the Chorus responded likewise, and as Antony's speech took hold, their responses shifted from individual responses to group responses. This emboldened Antony (and the actor playing him) and he brought his famous and powerful speech to a close with confidence and strength, leaving behind a very angry mob. As I experienced this from the audience, I could not help but be moved too.

SCENE 6 (ACT III, SCENE III)

The mob's angry energy from the previous scene carries directly into this scene, as they turn it toward the gentle Cinna the Poet. As mentioned previously, our production had Cinna accompanying the Soothsayer in earlier scenes as a sort of guide. I hoped that by contrasting a kind poet who helped the blind with a heartless and murderous mob, we would make Cinna's death more poignant.

At the end of the scene, with Cinna crumpled dead on the stage, the Soothsayer fumbled out with his cane, and upon discovering Cinna's body, dropped his cane and exited the stage in shock. I think this idea played better in concept than it did live because instead of feeling sorry for the two characters, and responding with a reverent silence, the audience laughed. I can't say why this happened, but there is a fine line between tragedy and comedy, and unexpected laughter is one of the perils of youth theater.

SCENE 7 (ACT IV, SCENE III)

The Chorus presents a very simple tableau to accompany Brutus's explanation that war is imminent. Holding swords, Chorus members raise their arms up in unison, point swords forward, and bring them down, settling in a military stance. Sometimes the simplest staging is the most effective at illustrating text or creating a mood.

By whispering the word "Brutus" in a wave from one chorus member to the other, down the chorus line and back, the Chorus provides a moody aural effect, aptly illustrating Caesar's ghost's spookiness. Throughout this production I was thrilled to discover for the first time how many wonderful theatrical effects a Chorus can create. I will most certainly try to find use for the Chorus in subsequent productions. The Chorus provides a way for actors who would otherwise only have minor parts to become integral to the play and appear in several scenes. This increases their importance in the production and solidifies the notion that the play is an ensemble piece.

Furthermore, by echoing key phrases verbally, and by physically illustrating the text through movement and tableaux, the Chorus makes it easier for audiences to follow the plot and themes of the play.

SCENE 8 (ACT V, SCENE III)

The actors playing Cassius and Pindarus run onto the stage as if being pursued by the enemy. They look out over the audience at an imaginary battlefield, breathing heavily. The players' commitment to the urgency and panic of war will bring life to this scene. In rehearsal, we created a tableau that depicted Pindarus and Cassius, watching from one side of the stage, viewing Titinius surrounded by cheering soldiers on the other. Pindarus and Cassius froze in an exaggerated physical expression of shock and dismay, turning away from what they mistakenly perceived to be Titinius's capture by Caesar's army. This gave the actors a physical image in rehearsal upon which to base their reactions on stage. Tableaux were so effective by the Chorus in this production that I used them as an effective rehearsal tool as well.

In our version, things did start to break down a little after Cassius's death. The actor playing Titinius made a strong acting choice by beginning to cry on her line, "Come Cassius's sword, and find Titinius's heart." Unfortunately, Brutus took a long time to enter, and Titinius apparently became bored with being dead—so she lifted her head and looked around for Brutus, to audience laughter. Furthermore, she had died on top of the already dead Cassius, who had started fidgeting around in an effort to get comfortable. We ended up with a small pile of squirming and impatient dead bodies that had now begun to giggle. The moment passed, however, and we were able to finish our tragedy with appropriate somberness.

SCENE 9 (ACT V, SCENE V)

This thirty-minute production of *Julius Caesar* is an ensemble piece in many ways, so it is fitting that it closes with the entire cast reciting the final lines in unison.

The Chorus emerges as a major player in the story, adding visual and aural enhancements at every step and providing a highly effective way to stage the crowd scenes. With the chorus at a 45-degree angle on either side of the stage or standing in a semicircle, the audience is treated to a play that comes at them directly and powerfully. Additionally, student actors who did not initially request a large role were able to contribute greatly to the play. The group worked as a team, and their dedication and commitment resulted in a *Julius Caesar* that was at once personal and universal. The cast tells a powerful tale, and as their reward, they own a piece of history.

Live theater is magical. It is the most dynamic form of entertainment available to us. There is nothing like the interchange between actors and audience, that vibrant energy that is created in the theater. Julius Caesar is surely one of the most powerful and enduring historical dramas ever written, and we are fortunate to be able to continue giving it life, especially with young performers who can give it the vitality it deserves.

* *JULIUS CAESAR:* SET AND PROP LIST

SET PIECES:

Chair

PROPS:

THROUGHOUT:

Swords

SCENE 1:

Walking stick for Soothsayer

SCENE 4:

Notebook for Cinna the Poet
Daggers for Conspirators

SCENE 6:

Notebook for Cinna the Poet
Sticks, swords, and clubs for Citizens
Walking stick for Soothsayer

SCENE 7:

Swords for Chorus

SCENE 8:

Dagger for Pindarus
Sword for Titinius

SCENE 9:

Sword for Brutus

Julius Caesar

By William Shakespeare

Performed by Banneker Academic High School
Mr. Bowman's Twelfth Grade English Class

Tuesday, March 20th 2012
Instructor: Mr. Leo Bowman | Guest Director: Mr. Nick Newlin

CAST:

Stage Manager: Kendra Hazel

Scene 1 (Act 1, Scene 2)
A Public Place

Narrator: Nijah Armstrong

Chorus stage right: Justice Harris, Olemeku Aledan, Nijah Armstrong, Janin Fuentes, Vondae Donaldson, Desirée Samuel (Chorus Leader)

Chorus stage left: Hassaan Ali (drums), Tracy Abraham, Tamika McKay, Diahna DeBruce, Rosa Martinez, Nikki Merchant

Caesar: Jevaughni Henry

Casca: Donae Owens

Calpurnia: Nzingha Massaquoi

Mark Antony: Kyree Rollins

Brutus: Markill Taylor

Cassius: Natia Contee

Soothsayer: Nijah Armstrong

Scene 2 (Act 2, Scene 1)
Brutus' orchard

Narrator: Diahna DeBruce

Chorus stage right: Justice Harris, Olemeku Aledan, Nijah Armstrong, Janin Fuentes, Vondae Donaldson, Desirée Samuel

Chorus stage left: Hassaan Ali (drums), Tracy Abraham, Tamika McKay, Diahna DeBruce,

Brutus: Markill Taylor

Decius Brutus: Quenice Simms

Trebonius: Rian Matthews

Cassius: Natia Contee

Cinna: Abosede Eniola

Metellus Cimber: Richy Carranza

Casca: Donae Owens

Portia: Bianca Kersellius

Scene 3 (Act 2, Scene 2)
Caesar's house

Narrator: Tamika McKay

Chorus stage right: Cherrie Coachman, Richy Carranza, Shalaya Crummie, Vondae Donaldson, Desirée Samuel

Chorus stage left: Abosede Eniola, Rian Matthews, Natia Contee, Donae Owens, Hassaan Ali (drums)

Caesar: Jevaughni Henry

Calpurnia: Nzingha Massaquoi

Decius Brutus: Quenice Simms

Scene 4 (Act 3, Scene 1)
Rome, before the Capitol

Narrator: Janin Fuentes

Soothsayer: Nijah Armstrong

Cinna the Poet: Shalaya Crummie

Citizens: Olemeku Aledan, Tamika McKay

Caesar: Jevaughni Henry

Metellus Cimber: Richy Carranza

Decius Brutus: Quenice Simms

Casca: Donae Owens

Cinna: Abosede Eniola

Trebonius: Rian Matthews

Brutus: Cherrie Coachman

Mark Antony: Kyree Rollins

Cassius: Natia Contee

Scene 5 (Act 3 Scene 2)
The Forum

Narrator: Bianca Kersellius

Chorus stage right: Justice Harris, Olemeku Aledan, Nijah Armstrong, Janin Fuentes, Vondae Donaldson, Nzingha Massaquoi, Desirée Samuel

Chorus stage left: Hassaan Ali (drums), Tracy Abraham, Tamika McKay, Diahna DeBruce, Rosa Martinez, Nikki Merchant, Donae Owens

Brutus: Cherrie Coachman

Mark Antony: Kyree Rollins

First Citizen: Justice Harris

Second Citizen: Diahna DeBruce

Third Citizen: Rosa Martinez

Fourth Citizen: Tamika McKay

Scene 6 (Act 3, Scene 3)
A street

Narrator: Donae Owens

Cinna the Poet: Shalaya Crummie

First Citizen: Justice Harris

Second Citizen: Diahna DeBruce

Third Citizen: Rosa Martinez

Fourth Citizen: Tamika McKay

Other citizens: Hassaan Ali, Vondae Donaldson, Nikki Merchant, Olemeku Aledan, Desirée Samuel, Tracy Abraham, Janin Fuentes

Scene 7 (Act 4. Scene 3)
Brutus' tent

Narrator: Rian Matthews

Chorus stage right: Markill Taylor, Desirée Samuel, Richy Carranza, Jevaughni Henry, Shalaya Crummie, Nzingha Massaquoi

Chorus stage left: Abosede Eniola, Olemeku Aledan, Rian Matthews, Donae Owens, Nikki Merchant, Bianca Kersellius

Brutus: Cherrie Coachman

Cassius: Natia Contee

Caesar's Ghost: Hassaan Ali

Scene 8: (Act 5, Scene 3)
The plains of Phillipi

Narrator: Quenice Simms

Brutus: Markill Taylor

Cassius: Natia Contee

Pindarus: Vondae Donaldson

Titinius: Nijah Armstrong

Messala: Olemeku Aledan

Strato: Janin Fuentes

Scene 9 (Act 5, Scene 5) another part of the battlefield

Narrator: Shalaya Crummie

Brutus: Markill Taylor

Clitus: Desirée Samuel

Messala: Olemeku Aledan

Volumnius: Tracy Abraham

Strato: Janin Fuentes

"The fault, dear Brutus, is not in our stars,
but in ourselves, that we are underlings."
—Cassius

ADDITIONAL RESOURCES

SHAKESPEARE

Shakespeare Set Free: Teaching Romeo and Juliet, Macbeth and a Midsummer Night's Dream
Peggy O'Brien, Ed., Teaching Shakespeare Institute
Washington Square Press
New York, 1993

Shakespeare Set Free: Teaching Hamlet and Henry IV, Part 1
Peggy O'Brien, Ed., Teaching Shakespeare Institute
Washington Square Press
New York, 1994

Shakespeare Set Free: Teaching Twelfth Night and Othello
Peggy O'Brien, Ed., Teaching Shakespeare Institute
Washington Square Press
New York, 1995

The *Shakespeare Set Free* series is an invaluable resource with lesson plans, activites, handouts, and excellent suggestions for rehearsing and performing Shakespeare plays in a classroom setting.

ShakesFear and How to Cure It!
Ralph Alan Cohen
Prestwick House, Inc.
Delaware, 2006

The Friendly Shakespeare: A Thoroughly Painless Guide to the Best of the Bard
Norrie Epstein
Penguin Books
New York, 1994

Brush Up Your Shakespeare!
Michael Macrone
Cader Books
New York, 1990

Shakespeare's Insults: Educating Your Wit
Wayne F. Hill and Cynthia J. Ottchen
Three Rivers Press
New York, 1991

Practical Approaches to Teaching Shakespeare
Peter Reynolds
Oxford University Press
New York, 1991

Scenes From Shakespeare: A Workbook for Actors
Robin J. Holt
McFarland and Co.
London, 1988

101 Theatre Games for Drama Teachers, Classroom Teachers & Directors
Mila Johansen
Players Press Inc.
California, 1994

THEATER AND PERFORMANCE

Impro: Improvisation and the Theatre
Keith Johnstone
Routledge Books
London, 1982

A Dictionary of Theatre Anthropology: The Secret Art of the Performer
Eugenio Barba and Nicola Savarese
Routledge
London, 1991

THEATER GAMES

Theatre Games for Young Performers
Maria C. Novelly
Meriwether Publishing
Colorado, 1990

Improvisation for the Theater
Viola Spolin
Northwestern University Press
Illinois, 1983

Theater Games for Rehearsal: A Director's Handbook
Viola Spolin
Northwestern University Press
Illinois, 1985

PLAY DIRECTING

Theater and the Adolescent Actor: Building a Successful School Program
Camille L. Poisson
Archon Books
Connecticut, 1994

Directing for the Theatre
W. David Sievers
Wm. C. Brown, Co.
Iowa, 1965

The Director's Vision: Play Direction from Analysis to Production
Louis E. Catron
Mayfield Publishing Co.
California, 1989

INTERNET RESOURCES

http://www.folger.edu
The Folger Shakespeare Library's website has lesson plans, primary sources, study guides, images, workshops, programs for teachers and students, and much more. The definitive Shakespeare website for educators, historians and all lovers of the Bard.

http://www.shakespeare.mit.edu.
The Complete Works of
William Shakespeare.
All complete scripts for *The 30-Minute Shakespeare* series were originally downloaded from this site before editing. Links to other internet resources.

http://www.LoMonico.com/Shakespeare-and-Media.htm
http://shakespeare-and-media.wikispaces.com
Michael LoMonico is Senior Consultant on National Education for the Folger Shakespeare Library. His *Seminar Shakespeare 2.0* offers a wealth of information on how to use exciting new approaches and online resources for teaching Shakespeare.

http://www.freesound.org.
A collaborative database of sounds and sound effects.

http://www.wordle.net.
A program for creating "word clouds" from the text that you provide. The clouds give greater prominence to words that appear more frequently in the source text.

http://www.opensourceshakespeare.org.
This site has good searching capacity.

http://shakespeare.palomar.edu/default.htm
Excellent links and searches

http://shakespeare.com/
Write like Shakespeare,
Poetry Machine, tag cloud

http://www.shakespeare-online.com/

http://www.bardweb.net/

http://www.rhymezone.com/shakespeare/
Good searchable word and phrase finder.
Or by lines:
http://www.rhymezone.com/shakespeare/toplines/

http://shakespeare.mcgill.ca/
Shakespeare and Performance research team

http://www.enotes.com/william-shakespeare

Needless to say, the internet goes on and on with valuable Shakespeare resources. The ones listed here are excellent starting points and will set you on your way in the great adventure that is Shakespeare.

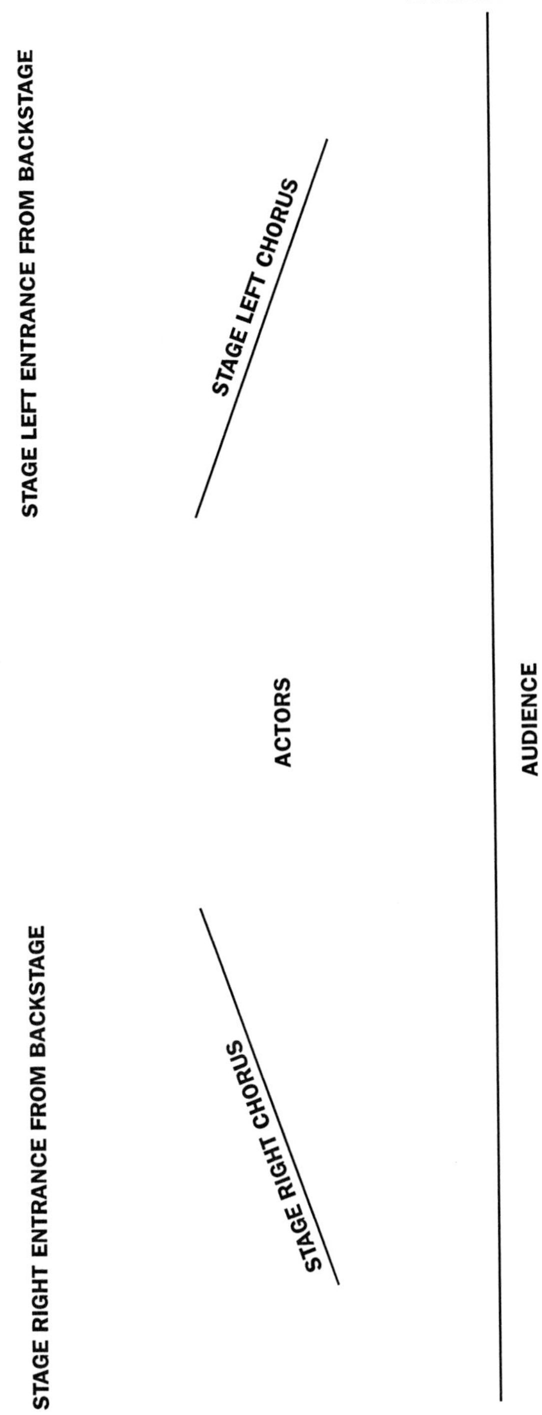
REAR ENTRANCE FROM BACKSTAGE
STAGE LEFT ENTRANCE FROM BACKSTAGE
STAGE RIGHT ENTRANCE FROM BACKSTAGE
STAGE LEFT CHORUS
ACTORS
STAGE RIGHT CHORUS
AUDIENCE

NICK NEWLIN has performed a comedy and variety act for international audiences for twenty-seven years. Since 1996, he has conducted an annual play directing residency affiliated with the Folger Shakespeare Library in Washington, D.C. Newlin received a BA with Honors from Harvard University in 1982 and an MA in Theater with an emphasis in Play Directing from the University of Maryland in 1996.

THE 30-MINUTE SHAKESPEARE

AS YOU LIKE IT
978-1-935550-06-8

THE COMEDY OF ERRORS
978-1-935550-08-2

HAMLET
978-1-935550-24-2

HENRY IV, PART 1
978-1-935550-11-2

JULIUS CAESAR
978-1-935550-29-7

KING LEAR
978-1-935550-09-9

LOVE'S LABOR'S LOST
978-1-935550-07-5

MACBETH
978-1-935550-02-0

A MIDSUMMER NIGHT'S DREAM
978-1-935550-00-6

THE MERRY WIVES OF WINDSOR
978-1-935550-05-1

MUCH ADO ABOUT NOTHING
978-1-935550-03-7

OTHELLO
978-1-935550-10-5

ROMEO AND JULIET
978-1-935550-01-3

THE TEMPEST
978-1-935550-28-0

TWELFTH NIGHT
978-1-935550-04-4

THE TWO GENTLEMEN OF VERONA
978-1-935550-25-9

All plays $7.95, available in print and eBook editions in bookstores everywhere

"A truly fun, emotional, and sometimes magical first experience . . . guided by a sagacious, knowledgeable, and intuitive educator." —Library Journal

CPSIA information can be obtained at www.ICGtesting.com
Printed in the USA
LVOW11s0234060914

402614LV00001B/3/P